NIDO R. QUBEIN

UNCOMMON SENSE

simple truths®
Your Destination For Inspiration
an imprint of Sourcebooks, Inc.

Ten Principles to Transform Your Work and Life

Editing by: Alice Patenaude

Photo Credits
Cover: designaart/Thinkstock
Internal: page 1, designaart/Thinkstock; page 3, Siarheyeva Veranika/Shutterstock; pages 8–9, Matt_Gibson/Thinkstock; page 10, Laura Flugga/Getty Images; page 12, Peter Bernik/Shutterstock; page 15, Hasloo Group Production Studio/Shutterstock; page 17, Zoonar RF/Thinkstock; pages 18–19, Bas Meelker/Thinkstock; page 20, anyaberkut/Thinkstock; page 22, David Broberg/Thinkstock; page 25, pixtawan/Thinkstock; pages 26–27, Olga Sapegina/Shutterstock; page 28, Iakov Kalinin/Thinkstock; page 33, Koca777/Thinkstock; page 35, ChamilleWhite/Thinkstock; pages 36–37, fotomak/Shutterstock; page 38, Nickolay Stanev/Shutterstock; page 41, wrangler/Shutterstock; page 43, High Point University; pages 44–45, Michael J. Ivins/Getty Images; page 46, David Kay/Shutterstock; page 49, Zurijeta/Thinkstock; pages 54–55, Epidote/Thinkstock; page 56, Ryan McVay/Thinkstock; page 58, Sandra Cunningham/Shutterstock; page 61, Rafal Olkis/Shutterstock; page 62, zirconicusso/Shutterstock; pages 64–65, Gordan/Shutterstock; page 66, PHOTOCREO Michal Bednarek/Shutterstock; page 69, Alfonso de Tomas/Shutterstock; page 71, jakelv7500/Shutterstock; pages 72–73, schalkc/Shutterstock; page 74, Daniela Pelazza/Shutterstock; page 77, Zurijeta/Shutterstock; page 78, Jose AS Reyes/Shutterstock; pages 80–81, Subbotina Anna/Shutterstock; page 82, NewSoul/Shutterstock; page 84, Neung Stock Enterprise/Shutterstock; page 87, wavebreakmedia/Shutterstock; page 89, Dudarev Mikhail/Shutterstock; pages 90–91, Huber-Images/Offset; page 92, hxdbzxy/Shutterstock; page 95, mangostock/Thinkstock; page 97, Stokkete/Shutterstock; page 99, MissHibiscus/iStock; pages 100–101, cmcderm1/iStock; pages 104–105, Sergey Nivens/Shutterstock

Published by Simple Truths, an imprint of Sourcebooks, Inc.
P.O. Box 4410, Naperville, Illinois 60567-4410
(630) 961-3900
Fax: (630) 961-2168
www.sourcebooks.com

Printed and bound in the United States of America.
WOZ 10 9 8 7 6 5 4 3 2 1

"Common sense in an **uncommon** degree is what the world calls **wisdom**."

—Samuel Taylor Coleridge

What Is **"Uncommon Sense,"** Anyway?

People tend to order their lives according to "conventional wisdom," a generally accepted set of principles that may include centuries-old folk sayings or that may have arisen from contemporary experience. These sayings and beliefs have become so ingrained in the public mind that they are often referred to as "common sense."

In both your business and your personal life, following conventional wisdom is usually the "safe" approach. But the people who make a remarkable difference in the world are typically those who examine conventional wisdom with a critical eye, using "uncommon sense."

Most people don't question conventional wisdom. It's just "the way things are." Others see it as a handy starting place for examining their own values. Using uncommon sense, they often discover wisdom that is far from conventional.

Somewhere along the way, someone questioned conventional wisdom, examined it from all sides, developed new principles, and produced human progress.

Common sense told the medieval world that the Earth was the center of the universe and the sun revolved around it. Copernicus followed uncommon sense to a new understanding of the universe and our place in it.

This book is not aimed at turning conventional wisdom on its head or debunking the wisdom of the ages. It seeks instead to encourage a creative look at things often taken for granted, to provide fresh insights into old verities.

Wise King Solomon wrote that the race is not always to the swift, nor the battle to the strong.

Damon Runyon added a footnote: "But that's the way to bet."

We often listen to conventional wisdom without paying much attention to the uncommon sense contained in the footnotes.

Yes, the tortoise of Aesop's fable crossed the finish line ahead of the hare. But it was a careless and negligent hare. The hare that keeps its focus on the race will outdistance the tortoise every time. "Fast and steady" will always win over "slow but sure."

I have lived long enough to acknowledge the value of wisdom based on generations of experience. I have also lived long enough to know that those who follow conventional wisdom uncritically may end up in a rut that leads nowhere.

So when I hear someone quote an old saying that suggests it's the wisdom of the ages, I start looking for footnotes and often find them with the nuggets of uncommon sense they contain. That sort of skeptical examination has served me well, and I recommend it to those who want to enjoy, discover, and achieve fulfillment in their lives.

Let me sound an immediate caveat: the advice I pass on in this book has worked for me. Whether it works for you will depend on the practical wisdom you show in applying it. Like all advice, it must be examined in the context of your own circumstances, aptitudes, personality, and aspirations. It is advice based on empirical—not clinical—evidence. I didn't acquire my background in a laboratory or clinic; I'm a businessperson and educator who has succeeded in a variety of endeavors.

In this book, I want to acquaint you with some of the guidelines I have followed in my own life. I have distilled them into ten uncommon principles.

The conventional explorer, in crossing a stream, may look at the stones rising from the water as islands of stability in the swirling current. And that they may be. But the creative explorer will stop and turn the stones over to determine whether priceless gems might lie beneath or what veins of gold might be incorporated in their mass.

Ancient adages are like those rocks in the stream, assuring the crosser that it's safe to step here. Those old saws serve a useful purpose. But unless we're willing to turn them over and look at the other side, we may never know what nuggets of wisdom, what omens of triumph, what uncommon principles lie underfoot. Let's turn a few stones. Let's examine some uncommon principles.

Enjoy this journey of inquisitive exploration.

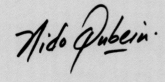

"Wisdom outweighs any wealth."
—Sophocles

COMMON PRINCIPLE **1**

Sharpen Your Information into Wisdom

Common sense:
Information is the raw material of achievement.

Uncommon sense:
Wisdom is information sharpened
into a useful tool.

"Wisdom is the principal thing," wrote the author of Proverbs. "Therefore, get wisdom: and with all thy getting get understanding."

As we explore the uncommon sense that leads to success, significance, and fulfillment in life, wisdom is the logical place to begin. Without wisdom, we are unlikely to take the measured steps required to build a satisfying future. We are unlikely to distinguish between sound counsel and faulty advice.

Exercising wisdom does not require super intellect; geniuses can act foolishly, and people of ordinary intelligence can act wisely. Wisdom does not require encyclopedic knowledge. A head full of information is like a dictionary full of words: just as the words in a dictionary can produce great literature or incoherent babble, the information in our heads may produce wise or irresponsible decisions.

Information without Wisdom Gets Us Nowhere

The world is awash with information. But information without wisdom gets us nowhere. When we're driving down a boulevard and see a traffic light ahead, we may discern that the signal is red. That's information. We know that the red signal means "stop." That's knowledge. But the information and knowledge won't help unless you apply your brakes and stop. That's wisdom.

Information is like food in the grocery store. The food does not become useful to us physically and nutritionally until we buy it, cook it, eat it, and digest it. Similarly, only when we absorb information, digest it, understand it, learn it, and act upon it does it provide nourishment for personal growth.

We're bombarded with information daily. It pours out of our radios, televisions, newspapers, magazines, books, DVDs, and the Internet. It's available at the turn of a knob, the push of a button, or the click of a mouse.

Information becomes knowledge as soon as it lodges in the brain. But wisdom takes longer to acquire.

Wisdom is uncommon sense—information sharpened into a useful tool. We begin with a body of information, then hone it and improve it. In time, the information develops into a reservoir of knowledge and, at some point, becomes wisdom. When we apply information and knowledge with wisdom, our words and actions influence others. We become persons of substance.

We Must **Acquire Knowledge**

Information is the foundation of wisdom. We can't act wisely without accurate information. Therefore, to influence others constructively, we must acquire knowledge.

Learning that leads to wisdom cannot be haphazardly obtained. It must be purposely sought, and the search for knowledge must be a continuum. Every day, before going to sleep, we should ask ourselves: What did I learn today that I did not know yesterday? Each bit of information obtained must fit into the fabric of knowledge already absorbed. By applying this knowledge to everyday challenges, we build up a body of experience, and that experience leads to wisdom.

Wisdom does not come from constant success; it comes from lessons learned through repeated failures. More than a century ago, Wilbur and Orville Wright tried to make something heavier than air fly through the atmosphere on a controlled path. Every failure seemed to tell them that man wasn't meant to fly, but it also told them what not to try next. Then, finally, something got them into the air, and modern aviation was off the ground.

As a university president, I'm fortunate to work side by side with stellar faculty who readily acknowledge that wisdom comes from innovative thinking, which leads to innovative action. To be innovative, we must, by definition, try new things. When we try anything new, we risk failure…but we must not allow that to deter us: failure can advance us toward our goals.

Productive Failure vs. Unproductive Success

Uncommon sense says that a productive failure is better than a nonproductive success. A productive failure is a failure that, upon analysis, teaches us something that can lead to future success. Nonproductive success is success that we achieve but don't know how we achieved it, and therefore we can't readily replicate it. We learn little or nothing from nonproductive successes.

Mark Twain is among many who have expressed the principle behind productive failures: "Good judgment comes from experience, and experience comes from bad judgment."

Thomas Edison made 1,000 bad judgments before he found the right filament for his lightbulb. He turned those bad judgments into productive failures. He gained wisdom from experiencing failure.

When your efforts result in failure, look for something you can learn from the situation that will later help you accomplish what you set out to accomplish.

Success May Be **One Failure Away**

But don't be too quick to proclaim failure. The obstacles that set us back may be only temporary snags. With applied wisdom, success may be only one failure away.

Acquire wisdom and treat it as the valuable asset it is. If all you have is information, people will use you and then discard you. If all you have is knowledge, people will need you until such a time as their own level of knowledge is equal to yours or in their view is sufficient. But if you have wisdom, people will respect you.

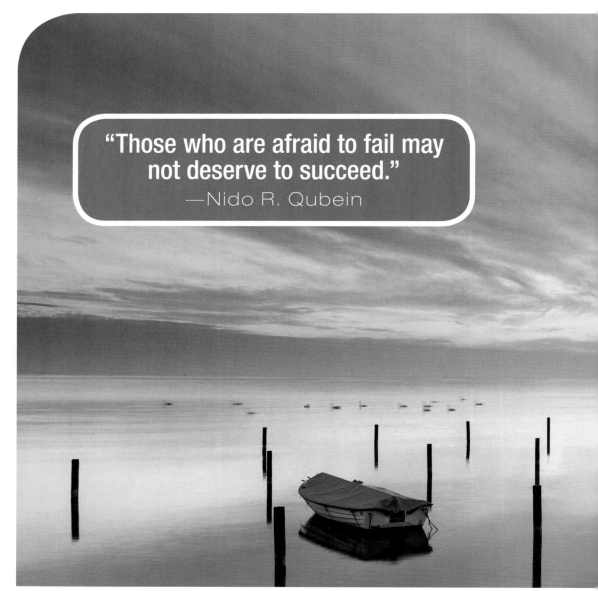

"Those who are afraid to fail may not deserve to succeed."
—Nido R. Qubein

UNCOMMON PRINCIPLE 2

Avoid the Urgent;
Focus on the
Important

Common sense:
Give priority to urgent tasks.

Uncommon sense:
Prevent tasks from becoming urgent.

One of the most important things achievers learn is how to distinguish between what is urgent and what is important.

The two are not the same.

Urgent choices are choices that demand immediate attention. Important choices are those that move us toward our goals. The fewer urgent choices we have, the more time and energy we have to focus on the important ones.

Obviously, to know whether a choice will move you closer to your goals, you must know what your goals are. That makes it important to form a clear vision of where you want to go. What represents success to you?

Vision Is a Thing of the Heart

People of accomplishment form vivid images of what things will be like once they have achieved what they want to achieve. They keep this vision in mind at all times. Vision is a thing of the heart. It's the desire that provides the energy and the will to keep going.

Goals are creatures of the mind. They are the intermediate steps on the way to the vision, mileposts on the way to success, significance, and fulfillment. To achieve our objectives, we must develop action plans—step-by-step procedures for reaching our goals.

Once a vision has been developed and goals established, we find it easier to distinguish the urgent from the important.

An urgent task may not be very important in the long run, but it demands immediate attention.

The danger is that in attending to the urgent task, we may neglect important tasks. Many people get so bogged down taking care of the urgent that they never find time for the important.

If the roof is leaking and water is dripping on your valuable armoire, the urgent task is to move the furniture. Moving the armoire doesn't solve the problem; it doesn't move you toward the goal of a weather-tight house. But if you don't move it, serious consequences occur. In the long run, though, the important task is to fix the roof.

You can avoid this dilemma by making sure the roof is kept in good repair. Common sense tells you to fix the roof when it starts leaking. Uncommon sense tells you to maintain your roof so it never starts leaking. You minimize urgent tasks by spotting problems while they're still minor and easily remedied and taking care of them at once. If you keep in perspective what's really important, you won't spend all your time doing what seems urgent.

What Is **Really Important?**

When we invest our lives in responding to urgencies, we allow circumstances and other people to choose how we will live. If we don't have a clearly focused objective to work on at any given moment, we're likely to spend our lives putting out brush fires. When we know what actions will move us closer to our objective, we can weigh the urgency against what is really important to us in the long run.

Problems left unaddressed will move through three stages: the proactive stage, at which they can be solved fairly simply; the reactive stage, at which remedial steps are necessary to turn the situation around; and the crisis stage, in which immediate action is required.

Some people seem to live constantly in the crisis phase. Others seem to go through life avoiding the rough times. How do they do it? By addressing problems while they're still in the proactive stage. This prevents unimportant things from turning into urgent situations that divert time and attention away from important things.

Sometimes you have to clear the decks of urgent matters by accepting the undesirable consequences and moving on. If paying the rent on your present place is driving you to the financial brink, it may be necessary to move into less expensive accommodations until your financial  situation has improved. It may be necessary to drive a less expensive car, eat out less often, and cut down on your entertainment budget.

These sacrifices require self-discipline, but you can muster it if you can see how the sacrifices will help you reach the goals that lead toward the glowing vision you have created.

"If you want to live a happy life, tie it to a goal, not to people or things."

—Albert Einstein

UNCOMMON PRINCIPLE 3

Manage Your Life,
Not Just Your Time

Common sense:
Time management makes each minute count.

Uncommon sense:
Life management makes your
whole existence count.

One of the topics I cover in The President's Seminar on Life Skills, a required course for all freshmen at High Point University, is time and energy management. Young people have an almost endless supply of energy, yet they have to learn to harness and focus their efforts to achieve worthwhile results.

If you're looking for a good Return on Life (ROL), then it's essential that you practice good life management—and that begins with energy management.

You've heard of time management: the arrangement of your daily activities in an orderly and efficient manner. Life management looks much farther ahead. Time management means knowing where you want to be at the end of the day and taking orderly steps to get there. Life management means deciding what you want on your tombstone and taking steps to make sure you earn the epitaph. Energy management ensures your battery doesn't run out before you accomplish your goals.

It means dreaming a large dream and aligning your actions with the dream. Time management may earn you a great day, a great week, or a great month. But to have a great life, you must be consistently great, and that requires long-term planning carried out with uncommon sense.

This doesn't mean that time management is not important. Many people never quite get around to life management because they never master the art of time management. They become so entangled in the minor details of getting through the day that they never get around to the major components of getting through life. Life management will help you put your accomplishments in logical, systematic order.

Start with Your Epitaph

To do that, you must start with the epitaph and work backward in time. Look down the road about twenty-five years. What do you want your life to be like then? To achieve that dream, what do you need to have accomplished twenty years from now? What about fifteen years? Ten years? Five years?

Organize your life's plan into these long-range and intermediate-range segments. To get where you need to be five years from now, what should you accomplish in the next year? To reach that one-year goal, what should you do in the next six months? The next month? The next week? Today?

Let your goals establish the order in which you do things. If an activity is important in relation to your goals, do it. If it's not, forget it and move on.

It's like **Painting a Picture**

I like to compare life management with the painting of a picture. Your painting starts as a sketch, an outline of what you propose to create. Without this outline, you will not exercise the discipline and control needed to achieve the desired end effect.

Your life also needs an outline, systems and structures that will enable you to discipline yourself to move toward the fulfillment of your vision.

The structures might include your job, your family, your community, and the organizations to which you belong. Systems would include your personal and professional habits, attitudes, behaviors, goals, and strategies.

When you're creating a painting, you are constantly making changes on the canvas. Each brush stroke is designed to improve what is there.

The same is true of your life. You must view your life as being in a state of constant improvement. Plan your actions purposely to improve what is already there.

Valuable Commodities

Life management means being purposeful in the way you invest your time, use your energy, and spend your money. All are valuable commodities, but there's one major difference: money is replaceable and energy is often replenishable, but time is not. Once you've spent it, you can't earn more.

Suppose you had $480,000. What would you do with it?

You probably wouldn't break it into small bills and hand it out indiscriminately to everyone you meet. You would probably look for ways to protect it and use it to accomplish constructive things.

From the ages of twenty to seventy-five, you have more than 480,000 hours to spend. You can't deposit them and expect them to draw interest. And you won't get them back. What will you do to make them yield the greatest return on your investment?

Isn't it ironic that some people protect their money and possessions with their lives, yet let their energy and time slip away with little thought? They don't seem to realize that time is their most valuable possession—the only part of their inventory that can never be replaced.

Let your deliberately chosen priorities dictate the way you spend your precious time and the way you manage your purpose-driven life. When you learn to plan your life around priorities, you will find yourself moving effectively toward your desired future. And you'll get the epitaph you want.

"Don't settle for style.
Succeed in substance."

—Wynton Marsalis

UNCOMMON PRINCIPLE 4

Reinforce Your Style with Substance

Common sense:
Style attracts.

Uncommon sense:
Substance retains.

A sprig of parsley enhances the appearance of a baked potato and makes it look more appetizing. But, if the potato is half-cooked or overcooked, the parsley won't make it palatable. The parsley may lead you to take the first bite, but if the potato is flawed, you won't take that second bite.

Think of the parsley as style and the potato as substance. In your personal and business lives you need both. But substance is more important by far. Style is the promise; substance is the delivery. If you don't deliver on your promise, whether it's implied or specific, people won't come back to you for more of what you offer.

Some people have the gift of charisma—that sparkling quality that causes others to respond to them favorably. But not all of them have substance behind the charisma. And, when people flock to them and discover that the substance isn't there, they turn away in disappointment, and often in anger. Charisma gets you in the door, but it takes substance to deliver results.

Don't try to put on a stylish front when there's no substance behind it. Be what you seem to be. And if the real you doesn't succeed, become what you need to be. Let me be clear: don't *act* like the person you need to be, *become* the person you need to be.

Businesses put a lot of money and effort into establishing brand names. But a clever brand name is no good unless it comes with a product that provides value as the customer perceives it. The same is true of individuals. People need to know that your name stands for value.

You can't achieve a positive personal brand by doing something. You can achieve it only by *being* something. And that something has to be authentic, recognizable, and purposeful.

To be authentic, you must consciously and intentionally bring your business, social, spiritual, and family lives into such harmony that a person looking at your performance in these roles will know what kind of person you really are.

When you've done that, you will have achieved a high level of substance people can rely on. Your personal brand will make a promise that your personal being will fulfill.

An Extraordinary **Education**

High Point University (HPU) is a practical case in point. Over the last decade, my team and I worked tirelessly to transform the institution and to create a culture where every student receives an extraordinary education in an inspiring environment with caring people.

We understood inherently that a beautiful campus with state-of-the-art facilities and technology (style) must be founded firmly on an educational program resourced with outstanding faculty, holistic and experiential learning, and measurable outcomes (substance). That's why our attention focused on small classes, meaningful programs, and values-based living. Today, HPU is ranked number one by *U.S. News & World Report* among Regional Colleges in the South.

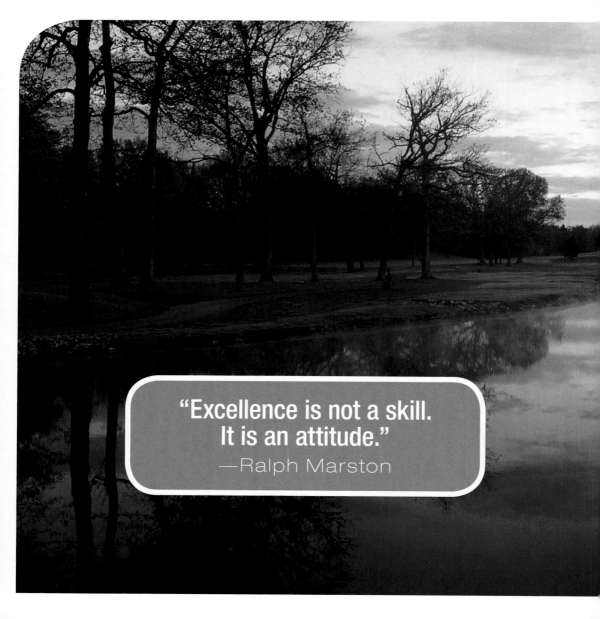

"Excellence is not a skill.
It is an attitude."
—Ralph Marston

UNCOMMON PRINCIPLE 5

Don't Just Improve; Excel!

Common sense:
There's always room for improvement.

G

Uncommon sense:
Always make room for excellence.

If you want to achieve success, significance, and fulfillment, don't be satisfied with improvement.

If you're in last place and you move up to next to last, you've improved. But, you're not likely to go home and brag about it.

The standard to aim for is excellence, not improvement. Improvement is to excellence what grape juice is to champagne: an intermediate step on the way from the vine to the glass. You don't aim for the juice; you aim for the bubbly. Whatever your endeavor is, make excellence the standard by which you judge your performance.

The quest for excellence is an inward one. You won't find it in a book, in a seminar, or in an expensive piece of high-tech equipment. You'll find it within yourself.

Excellence is a quality of heart and soul, not of mechanical processes. As Elbert Hubbard, prolific writer, publisher, artist, and philosopher of the late nineteenth and early twentieth centuries, put it: "One machine can do the work of fifty ordinary [people]. No machine can do the work of one extraordinary [person]."

Excellence is the quality that distinguishes the extraordinary from the ordinary. In the modern business world, excellence is often equated with being free from defects. Some people regard that as an unrealistic goal. They're happy if their product is 99 percent free of defects.

But how would you like it if your phone went dead for fifteen minutes each day? How would you feel if you found three misspelled words on each page of this book? What kind of confidence would you feel in your hospital if you knew that doctors and nurses nationwide dropped 35,000 newborn babies a year? Would you trust your local pharmacist if you knew that 200,000 people get the wrong prescriptions every day?

That's what the 99 percent standard will get you. The person committed to excellence will not be happy with anything less than 100 percent.

But even being free from defects doesn't guarantee excellence. A Model T free from defects is still a Model T. Though it represented excellence in its day, it cannot match the extraordinary quality of today's luxury cars.

In our demanding and competitive world, quality means providing customers with the products and services they want the way they want them, no hassles, no errors. Excellence means doing that to an extraordinary degree.

Cultivate **Your Excellence**

In today's global market, we cannot afford to produce shoddy goods and render substandard services. The pursuit of excellence on a global scale means that second-rate performance cannot be tolerated. Either we produce at top quality or we become part of an inglorious history.

Aristotle said, "We are what we repeatedly do. Excellence, then, is not an act, but a habit." It's a habit that we acquire through training and habituation.

You can acquire the habit of excellence by cultivating these five qualities:

TEACHABILITY

Be open to new ideas and new ways of doing things. Be willing to listen, observe, and learn constantly.

ADAPTABILITY

Be willing to adjust to constant change.

FLEXIBILITY

Be willing to work smoothly with people of many different talents, temperaments, and personalities.

CREATIVITY

Try new things, building on your successes and learning from your mistakes.

SENSITIVITY

Be aware of the needs, interests, and concerns of others, including coworkers, clients, and patrons.

We pick up habits from the crowd we associate with. If our companions are sloppy and lax, we're likely to pick up their bad habits. If they insist on the best, their taste for excellence will rub off on us.

So whatever it is you do, seek out the people who do it best. Observe the people who excel at their jobs. Ask for their advice and follow their examples.

Extraordinary Performers

Don't wait until you need help with a problem to seek advice from the best. Studies have shown an interesting difference between ordinary and extraordinary performers. Ordinary performers wait until they need help. Then, they go looking for the people whose expertise they need. Extraordinary performers cultivate friend-ships with the experts before they need the expertise. Then, when they need the help, it's readily available.

Look for and develop your "differential advantage." Your differential advantage is something you can do better than anybody else to meet the needs of the people around you. It may come from doing things faster, cheaper, more skillfully, or more thoroughly than any of your competitors. It may come from having more experience, more specific knowledge, or more convenient locations. It may come from being the biggest, the most flexible, or the most accessible of all the companies in your business.

Whatever it is, find it and exploit it. Your differential advantage is your ticket to excellence.

Now, let's say a word on behalf of improvement. Rarely do people move from mediocrity to excellence in one giant step. They get there by taking numerous small steps. That's improvement. But the small improvements you make day-by-day can accumulate like compounded interest. Eventually they'll add up to excellence.

Every improvement in life is the result of change. All meaningful change comes from within. For the confident, change is opportunity.

You don't have to be a superhero to achieve excellence. All you need is a commitment to do more than ordinary people do—and do it consistently, in spite of the bumps in the road. Make that commitment today and follow it to your promising future.

"There are no unrealistic dreams, just unrealistic timelines."

—Nido R. Qubein

UNCOMMON PRINCIPLE 6

Put Your ROL Ahead of Your Net Worth

Common sense:
Return on investment is a way to measure profit.

Uncommon sense:
Return on life is a way to measure
significance, impact, and fulfillment.

If you want to get rich quickly, link up with a drug cartel. You'll start making money hand over fist. Your return on investment (ROI) may be astronomical.

But will you find success, significance, and fulfillment?

Many people equate success with wealth, but if you suggest that they amass their wealth through drugs, or even through illegal stock market tactics, the idea will repel most of them. Such routes to wealth may lead to a lavish lifestyle, but you'll forfeit your self-respect, your good name, your good conscience, perhaps your freedom, and maybe even your life.

Truly successful people know that there's something more important than ROI. It's ROL, Return on Life. ROI is what we get back from investing money. ROL is what we get back from investing ourselves.

Life is a wonderful opportunity to do good and to be good—to do more so we can have more, so we can give more. The biblical adage "it is better to give than to receive" is demonstrably true.

People who have achieved success, significance, and fulfillment know the satisfaction of seeing their efforts bear fruit far beyond their own personal lives. Uncommon sense says that the most gifted composer on Earth would get little satisfaction from playing his compositions only for himself. The most gifted actor needs an audience to achieve real fulfillment. People who achieve great wealth find their riches will provide little comfort if they, and only they, benefit from them.

Balance Your Life

Success can be defined in one word: balance. We become success-ful when we have achieved spiritual, familial, mental, physical, social, and economic balance. When we achieve this bal-ance, we feel joy and comfort. A truly balanced person keeps expanding intellectually, interacts effectively with other people, seeks constant spiritual growth, cultivates physical fitness, maintains a healthy family environment, and guarantees economic well-being.

Once we're balanced in all these areas, ROL will be high indeed.

Balanced people are other-oriented, constantly looking for ways to improve the world they live in and for ways to attract the support of people who will help them. When you're balanced, you don't wait for opportunities to serve your fellow humans. You look for them.

Achieving Balance

Here's a good formula for achieving balance in life:

- Invest a third of your life in earning; you must have resources if you want to be able to give resources.

- Invest a third of your life in learning; read books and periodicals every week.

- Invest one third of your life in giving and service.

Cultivate a love for learning and a capacity for earning. These qualities are important ingredients for life. But the things people really are passionate about are those that come directly from their sense of service. We tend to concentrate our energy in these things, to stay the course with them, because they have a depth of meaning in our lives.

Purpose in Life Is the Most Exciting Experience

Some people look for excitement through sports, entertainment, or an active social life. Each of these sources of pleasure has a place in the balanced life. But the excitement that produces ROL comes from inside. It's the excitement that results from reaching for a dream and pursuing it, of losing ourselves in a greater cause.

Anyone can have such a dream. It arises from deep inside, from the very essence of who we are.

Find yours, and make it your life's vision. Make it exciting and challenging—something that will bring forth the best within you. And make it something that will compel people to think of you with gratitude long after you're gone.

The Purpose Level

Some people lead their lives a task at a time, without meditating on where the series of tasks is taking them. Some live at the goal level, aiming toward short-term objectives without thinking of the big picture. But the happiest people are those who live their lives at the purpose level.

A bricklayer who thinks about only one brick at a time may or may not finish the wall, depending on whether he needs the pay and how many obstacles he encounters in building it. A bricklayer who envisions the finished edifice will show up regardless of the obstacles he encounters and regardless of whether he needs the money. He is committed to a purpose larger than himself. He has a winner's attitude. He has uncommon sense.

"One of the keys to effective leadership," observed Robert D. Bates, an insurance executive, "is operating with what I call 'bloodstream beliefs.' It's not just that we believe in these values; they're in our blood. We can't not do them because they're so central to who we are."

Identify your "bloodstream beliefs." Use them as the foundation of your life's purpose. Make that purpose one that will benefit our world. Then invest yourself fully in it. You'll be delighted with your ROL.

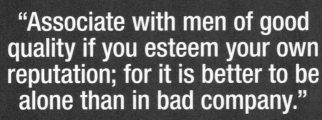

"Associate with men of good quality if you esteem your own reputation; for it is better to be alone than in bad company."

—George Washington

Lie Down with Well-Bred Dogs

Common sense:
Lie down with dogs, get up with fleas.

Uncommon sense:
Run with the top dogs,
come home with the bone.

It's been said that "if you lie down with dogs, you'll get up with fleas."

That's true only if the dogs are flea-bitten. If you lie down with dogs that are well-bred, well-trained, accomplished hunters, you may learn how to bring home the game.

My mother taught me when I was very young, "Who you spend time with is who you become." Those who associate with achievers are very likely to end up acting and thinking like achievers and will probably become achievers. Make sure the friends you associate with have positive attitudes and good habits. Cultivate these friends not because of what they can do for you, but because of what you can learn from them.

If you want to be great, you must first walk hand in hand and side by side with great people. You must not only walk with them, but also study them, emulating their successes and learning from their mistakes. You can walk with great people through personal acquaintance and through reading their biographies. Their examples can help you to recognize and analyze the failures in your own life and to extract from them ideas and procedures for doing better the next time.

Have Your **Knowledge in Order**

Mother used to tell me that I should always learn from experts because they have their knowledge in order. Look for people who have their knowledge in order—business people and industrialists, community leaders, and philanthropists—from whom you can learn all kinds of principles for insightful living.

When we associate with leaders, we tend to aim high, because our associates aim high. We need the company of the best to stretch us toward higher achievement.

Citation, one of the greatest thoroughbreds of all time, kept fast company during his racing days. Trainer Ben Jones once told jockey Eddie Arcaro, "Eddie, any horse Citation can see, he can catch. And he's got perfect eyesight."

Other horses have circled the track in less time than the 1948 Triple Crown winner. But Citation fans are convinced that the great horse could have overtaken the fastest, had they been on the same track at the same time. When you run with the best, you stretch yourself to keep up with the best.

Those of us who grew up in homes where good habits were modeled and nurtured find it easier to acquire positive habits. The discipline to develop them is part of our everyday environment.

Those who are not so fortunate must look for environments that will allow them to cultivate good habits.

Such environments may be found in the many organizations and interest groups that exist in every community. Service clubs such as Rotary, Kiwanis, and the Jaycees offer grassroots opportunities to mingle with leaders and to develop and exercise leadership qualities. Heading up a Lions Club broom sale may not rank high on the scale of influential positions, but it is a ground-floor entry into the world of leadership.

When it comes to choosing friends, it pays to aim high.

"You give but little when you give of your possessions. It is when you give of yourself that you truly give."
—Kahlil Gibran

UNCOMMON PRINCIPLE 8

Don't Give Back,

Just Give

Common sense:
It's better to give than to receive.

☙

Uncommon sense:
It's better to give than to give back.

To measure a person's worth as a human being, don't look at the level of earnings—look at the level of giving. Our value to humanity depends on how much of ourselves we give to make the world a better place.

Sometimes people explain an act of charity with the statement, "This community has been good to me, and I want to give something back to it."

That's a nice attitude, but it raises the question: Would such benefactors be so generous if they didn't feel indebted to the community? Would they allow a need to go unfilled simply because they owed the community nothing?

A Zero-Sum Equation

True generosity involves giving, not just giving back. It means giving with no expectation of repayment. Giving back is a zero-sum equation: We give back what we received, and the world is not better off than it was before we received it. True giving means the world is improved by the sum of our giving. It is better off because we are here.

People who view their stewardship in a role of giving back miss the point. To be significant in your world, we must focus on giving, period. Not giving back. Not giving as a payment. Just giving because there's a need we can fill and we want to fill it.

It's the kind of giving exemplified by the Good Samaritan of Jesus's parable who found a stranger in distress, poured medicinal wine on his wounds, took him to an inn, and paid the innkeeper to care for him, with a promise to pay more if that didn't meet all his needs. The

Samaritan didn't know the stranger by the roadside. He owed him nothing. He asked nothing in return. He gave out of the goodness of his soul.

"Always give without remembering. Always receive without forgetting," said William Barclay, the Scottish theologian. That's a wonderful attitude.

Giving rewards the giver much more than giving back. The most gratifying reward comes when we give not because we have to, not because someone asks us to, not because we owe it, but rather out of hearts filled with gratitude.

People whose hearts are full of gratitude tend to be more positive, generous, and innovative. They also tend to be easier to get along with—and therefore, more successful and influential.

Unconditional giving is like parental loving at its best. Good parents don't love their children because the children love them first. They don't "love back" their children. They love their children—period—even though the children at times may seem unlovable.

Many Avenues of Giving

The good news is that we don't have to own fortunes to give generously. There are many ways we can give, even though we may be lacking in financial resources. We can give talent, skill, time, or love; we can mentor, coach, advise, guide, or serve someone as a role model. These are all avenues of giving.

Giving back is not, in itself, a bad thing. But when we graduate from giving back to just giving, we arrive at the zenith of true pleasure. Go there and see for yourself!

"Set peace of mind as your highest goal and organize your life around it."
—Brian Tracy

Turn Happiness into Fulfillment

Common sense:
Happiness is the ultimate goal in life.

Uncommon sense:
Happiness is to fulfillment what Internet
chat rooms are to human conversation.

Some people devote their lives to the pursuit of happiness. They would be better off seeking fulfillment.

Happiness is a thing of the moment. Fulfillment is lasting. You can feel happy one minute and sad the next. But if you feel fulfilled, the good feeling remains, because fulfillment means you've made a mark that won't be erased.

Happiness is to fulfillment as chat rooms are to in-person conversations. Happiness is to fulfillment as virtual reality is to reality. Go for the real thing. Seek reality. Make your conversations face-to-face.

Some people try to use money to achieve happiness. If they use the money selfishly and unwisely, they'll have nothing left when it's gone, and they'll be unfulfilled. Some people base their future on good looks or good health. But age has a way of eroding both, and if that's your goal, you're surely headed toward an unfulfilled life.

Sense of **Gratification**

Fulfillment comes from a life well-lived—a life devoted to making the world a better place. When you make the world a better place to live, you become a better person. You are filled with a great sense of gratification.

When the final books are balanced, our reward isn't measured by the size of the estate we've amassed, the prestigious connections we've cultivated, or the famous awards we've won. It will be measured by the number of people we have helped, the legacy we have left, the stewardship we are invested in, the philanthropy we have extended, and the seeds we've planted in the lives of others. When those seeds germinate and grow, the people in whom we plant them can, in a significantly wonderful way, go out and do something worthwhile in their own lives. The way we multiply and leverage ourselves is through other people. That is why successful and significant people become engaged in areas of life that really have little to do with building riches. In fact, such worthwhile activities may cost them money. The truly successful become involved in the civic life of their communities. They use their wealth to provide opportunities for others. They use their time in the service of their neighborhoods.

Fruits of **Your Efforts**

When you provide a young person with an opportunity to go to college, you gain a sense of fulfillment that won't go away. When your efforts enhance the beauty, health, or economic security of your community, you have accomplished something that is rewarding to you, as well as to those who enjoy the fruits of your efforts.

Accomplishments such as these bring a much greater sense of purpose than just making money or accumulating awards.

Self-interest is a wonderful thing, but enlightened self-interest is ten times better. It's not about what we get; it's really about what we give.

Some people never learn the difference between fulfillment and fun. Fun is momentary. Joy is everlasting. Fulfillment is enduring.

Some people, mistaking fun for fulfillment, spend all their time having a ball. Often, they have nothing to go home to after the ball is over. Life can't be one continuous party. True happiness can be achieved only by building a solid foundation for success, significance, and fulfillment.

Searching for Happiness Is Self-Defeating

One classic myth is that a person will "find" happiness at a future time—a "magic moment"—and usually in a distant place. Yet, as psychiatrist Viktor E. Frankl said, "Happiness cannot be pursued; it must ensue." Those who spend their lives searching for happiness never find it, while those who establish a pattern of meaning, purpose, and strong personal relationships find that fulfillment usually comes to them as a by-product of those three things.

Ask yourself this question: "If I were to die tomorrow, what would I most regret not having done?"

Face it: You're not likely to die tomorrow. What's keeping you from doing the thing you would most regret not doing?

Do it, and you will be on the road to fulfillment.

GGGGGGGGGGGGGGGGGGGGGGGGGGGGGGGGGGGGGGGGGGGGGGGGGGG Turn Happiness into **Fulfillment**

"The purpose of life is a life of purpose."
—Robert Byrne

Legacy before
Fame and Fortune

Common sense:
Fame and fortune are temporary.

❡

Uncommon sense:
A legacy is forever.

Many people have made fame and fortune the Holy Grail of their existence. They pursue both with single-minded purpose.

It's better to leave a legacy.

Fame has a seductive glitter that makes people want to pursue it. But once they have it, it often turns to dust. Fortune, when employed in the service of mankind, can be a blessing. Yet when expended on selfish pursuits, it more often proves to be a curse.

Princess Diana achieved instant fame when she married Britain's Prince Charles, but she found the royal palaces to be restrictive. Elvis Presley rose from humble beginnings to become one of the most recognized figures on the planet, but fame and fortune did not bring him peace and fulfillment. Howard Hughes became one of the richest men on earth, with Hollywood queens for consorts. But he died a lonely recluse.

We could cite hundreds of examples of people who became entertainment idols, athletic heroes, business tycoons, and political successes without achieving the goals of fulfillment, satisfaction, and a sense of achievement.

Fame and fortune are fleeting. Time dims the memory of who we were and what we did. Fortunes can evaporate, and even if they don't, we can't take them to the grave.

VOLUNTEER

VOLUNTEER

DONATION
BOX

What's Your **Legacy?**

A legacy is what you bequeath to humanity. If it's a good legacy, its benefits will remain long after your name has been forgotten. Your family will rejoice in it. And you'll have invested your energy in helping to build a better world.

What your legacy is depends on what you choose to put at the center of your life. You can make riches and fame your twin goals. Or, you can choose to make this planet a better place for everything on it.

Before he was thirty, Albert Schweitzer won worldwide fame as a theologian, as an organist and authority on organ-building, and as an expert on Johann Sebastian Bach. But he is remembered today for founding a hospital in the remote backwoods of Gabon in West Africa. That is his legacy.

When I was a student in college, I worked ten hours a day to pay for my schooling. At the end of my last year, the college president told me there was a gap between what I paid and what I owed the school.

"You might want to know, a doctor in a neighboring city paid the difference," he said.

I wanted to know who my benefactor was, but he wished to remain anonymous. To this day, I don't know his identity. But I am a part of his legacy.

Start Your Legacy Now

Don't make fame and fortune your principal goals in life. Fame can be an impediment, and fortune should be a means to a greater end. By all means, pursue financial success. It can provide muscle to build a legacy. But don't wait until you're rich to start building that legacy. Had Mother Teresa waited until she was rich to start doing good, the poor people of India never would have felt her loving touch.

The way we multiply and leverage ourselves is through other people. It may have nothing to do with making money; if anything, it may cost money. But making money and receiving prestigious awards are not the highest goals in life. Life is about purpose. It's about fulfillment.

GGG

Once you've built that fortune, and perhaps achieved your fame, remember that fame and fortune have short shelf lives. Look for good things you can do that will remain long after you're gone. If Albert Schweitzer had been content with fame and fortune, he never would have left the concert halls of Europe, and the world by now would have forgotten him.

"I believe that being successful means having a balance of success stories across the many areas of your life. You can't truly be considered successful in your business life if your home life is in shambles."

—Zig Ziglar

A Word of **Encouragement**

I have just shared with you some of the principles that have enabled me to fulfill many of my dreams in life. I have benefited from the unselfish generosity of many people, some I never knew. But their generosity would have gone for naught had I not made positive and constructive use of it. I hope you will make fruitful use of the ideas in this book.

Here are some of the major points I hope you'll remember:

- Success does not guarantee joy. To turn success into joy, add significance and fulfillment.

- Success, significance, and achievement don't depend on what we do; they depend on who we are.

- The truly generous don't give back; they just give.

- In the long run, a noble legacy is more important than fame or fortune.

- The life worth living is the life in which spiritual, mental, social, physical, intellectual, and economical dimensions are in congruence.

- Don't seek improvement; seek excellence.

- Don't waste energy on things that don't matter or over which you have no control.

- Income is temporary; value is permanent.

- Don't sell without serving.

- Big things consist of many little things—and you have to achieve the little things first.

May the application of these uncommon principles lead you to uncommon success, significance, and fulfillment. All things are possible for those with faithful courage!

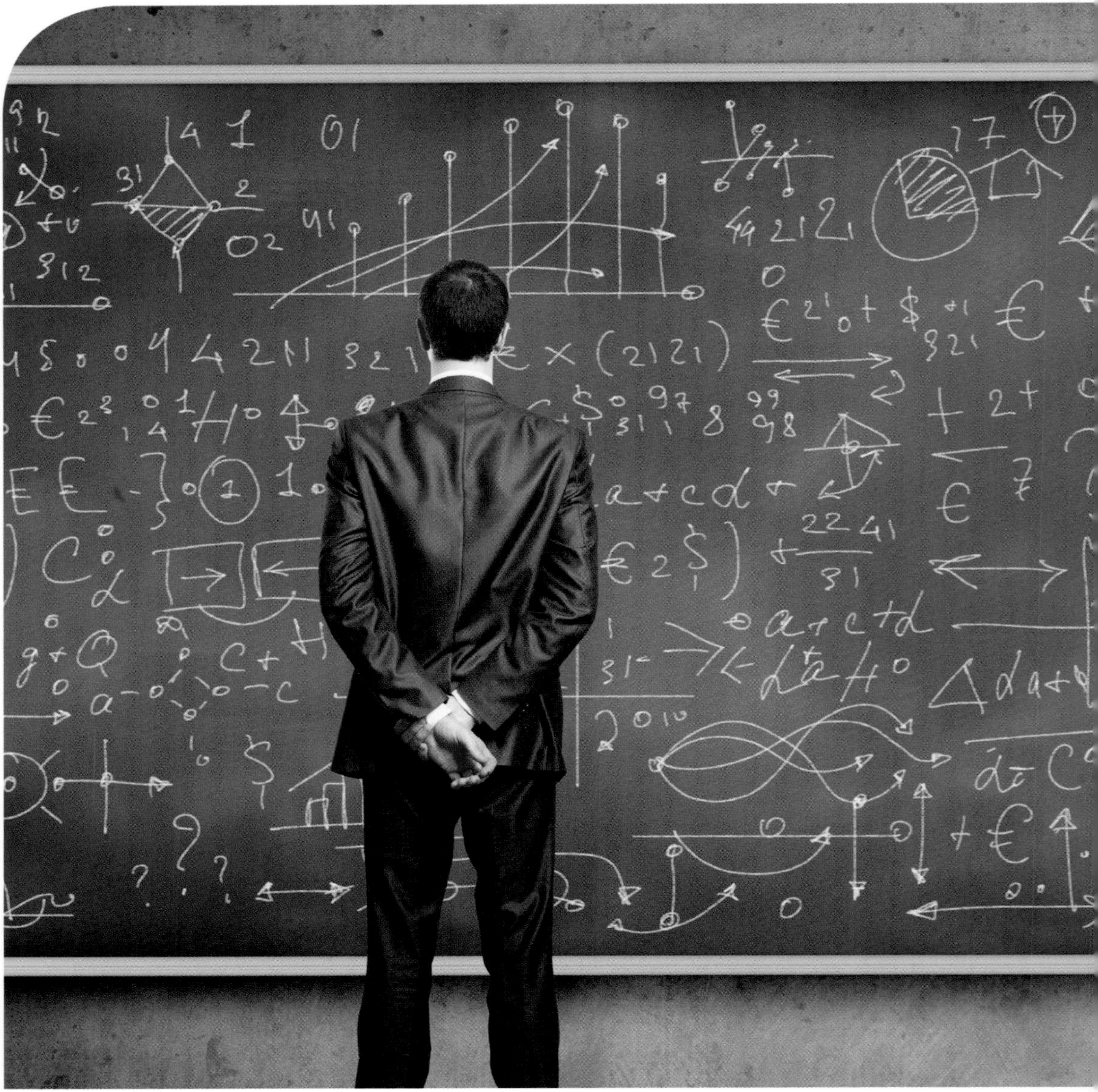

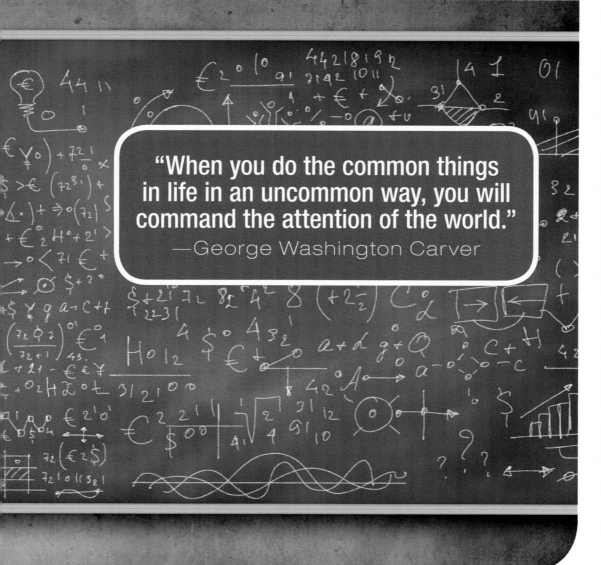

"When you do the common things in life in an uncommon way, you will command the attention of the world."

—George Washington Carver

About the **Author**

Nido R. Qubein came to the United States as a teenager with limited knowledge of English and only fifty dollars in his pocket. His inspiring life story is one filled with both adversity and abundance. It is through the lens of his life's journey that one appreciates his current role as an educator, philanthropist, and passionate advocate for the development of future leaders.

Dr. Qubein has served as the seventh president of High Point University since 2005, leading the university through an extraordinary transformation that includes tripling enrollment and the number of faculty, as well as the construction of fifty-five new buildings on campus. Under his leadership, four academic schools have been added: Communication, Health Sciences, Art and Design, and Pharmacy. HPU's rankings moved from number seventeen to number one in Regional Colleges in the South among America's Best Colleges 2013 and 2014 by *U.S. News & World Report*. Additionally, *U.S. News & World Report* ranks HPU number one in Undergraduate Teaching in the South for 2014.

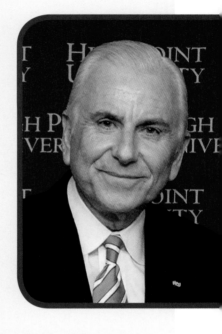

Prior to accepting his role as the president of High Point University, Dr. Qubein served as chairman of a consulting firm with clients in business and professional services. He is the recipient of the highest awards, including the Cavett (known as the Oscar of professional speaking), the Speakers Hall of Fame, the Horatio Alger Award for Distinguished Americans, the Ellis Island Medal of Honor, the Daughters of the American

Revolution's Americanism Award, and Sales and Marketing International's Ambassador of Free Enterprise. Toastmasters International named him the Top Business and Commerce Speaker and awarded him the Golden Gavel Medal. Dr. Qubein has also been inducted into Beta Gamma Sigma, the honor society for business leadership.

He served as president of the National Speakers Association, which has a membership of 4,000 professionals, and is the founder of the National Speakers Association Foundation, where the highest award for philanthropy is named after him.

His business experience led him to help grow a bank in 1986, and today, he serves on the board and the executive committee of BB&T Corporation, a Fortune 500 company with $185 billion in assets and 35,000 employees. Dr. Qubein is also chairman of Great Harvest Bread Company, with 224 stores in forty-two states, and serves on the board of La-Z-Boy Incorporated, one of the world's largest and most recognized furniture retailers. He serves as a director of Dots, a national chain of 450 women's apparel stores, and is a former trustee of the YMCA of the USA, which oversees more than 2,600 YMCAs across the country.

He has written a dozen books and recorded scores of audio and video learning programs. Dr. Qubein is an active speaker and consultant addressing business and professional groups across North America.

You can reach him at **nqubein@highpoint.edu** or visit his website, **www.nidoqubein.com.**

Dr. Nido R. Qubein became the seventh president of High Point University in January 2005. Since that time, President Qubein has partnered with faculty and staff to forge new opportunities for HPU. Focusing on experiential education and holistic, values-based learning, graduates are truly prepared to live a life of both success and significance. The numbers tell the story:

	2005	2013	GROWTH
Undergraduate Enrollment	1450	4000	176%
Full-Time Faculty	108	260	140%
Campus Size (Acres)	92	370	302%
Square Footage	800,000	3 million	275%
Buildings on Campus	22	107	386%
Total Positions	430	1309	204%
Economic Impact	$160.3 million	$464.5 million	190%
Operating Budget	$38 million	$178 million	368%
United Way Giving	$38,000	$200,000	426%
Study Abroad Programs	5	41	720%

Under Dr. Qubein's leadership, HPU has delivered on its simple, yet profound promise to students and their families:

*At High Point University, every student receives an extraordinary education in an inspiring environment with caring people.*SM

We invite you to visit and see for yourself this extraordinary place.

HIGH POINT UNIVERSITY

833 Montlieu Ave.
High Point, NC 27262
highpoint.edu
800-345-6993

simple truths®
THE GIFT OF INSPIRATION

You Can't
SALES MOTIVATION
CHANGE IS GOOD...
ROBIN CROW
THE POWER OF
The Richest
FINISH STRONG
by Dan Green
212°
The POWER OF ATTITUDE
MAC ANDERSON
The ESSENCE OF LEADERSHIP
MAC ANDERSON
Simple Secrets to a Happy Life